Original title:
Leaf Me Alone

Copyright © 2025 Creative Arts Management OÜ
All rights reserved.

Author: Liam Sterling
ISBN HARDBACK: 978-1-80566-605-9
ISBN PAPERBACK: 978-1-80566-890-9

Green Fractals of Dissonance

In the park, I take a seat,
Under branches soft and sweet.
Whispers rustle, leaves take flight,
Like my sanity, out of sight.

A squirrel jokes, such cheeky glee,
It taunts me from a nearby tree.
While acorns drop with playful sound,
I'm not laughing, just confound.

Unraveled Twirls

Spinning like a silly top,
I twirl and tipped, just can't stop.
Around me twigs like dancers play,
In this leafy cabaret.

Chasing shadows, losing track,
As nature teases with its knack.
Lost my hat, it's flown away,
To join the dance, that's just my day!

A Quiet Retreat

In my nook, I sip my tea,
Branches talk, just to mock me.
They giggle softly, shake and sway,
Like they've got something to say.

A critter peeks, then darts with fright,
Is it me or the falling light?
I ponder sips of quiet bliss,
But nature brings its leafy twist.

Breathing in the Abyss

With each breath, a leaf does fall,
It lands on me, it's nature's call.
'Come join us!' they seem to say,
'In the mess of this glorious play!'

But I just want a moment's peace,
From all this rustle, mayhem, and fees.
Yet laughter echoes through the trees,
And here I am, the jester's tease!

Boughs of Discord

In a tree full of chatter, it's quite a sight,
Branches argue loudly, it's quite a fright!
Squirrels throw nuts, like pebbles in war,
While birds start a chorus, that none can ignore.

The leaves start to gossip, oh what a show,
Whispering secrets that only they know.
The roots roll their eyes, and just shake their heads,
Thinking, 'Why can't these branches just go to their beds?'

Twirling Away

There was a twig who fancied a dance,
Spinning around without a chance.
Dizzy and dizzy, he took a fall,
Bouncing off bark, then crashing through all.

The wind laughed and teased, saying 'Look at him twirl!'
As he got caught up in a bright leafy whirl.
He screamed up to clouds, 'Now this is too much!'
But the humor in chaos was hard to touch.'

Rust and Ruin

A couple of leaves, in a ratty old heap,
Whispered of glory when they were a leap.
But rust had crept in, their shine had all dimmed,
Now they joke of the time they could almost swim.

The bark gives a chuckle, 'You were quite the sight!'
But their memories fade, as they cling to their plight.
Yet in this decay, they find ways to jest,
Poking fun at the trees, who now look their best.

The Lengthening Shadows

As shadows grow long on a bright sunny day,
The trees start to stretch in a comical way.
They bend and they twist, like dancers on stage,
Making little kids giggle and birds disengage.

A grasshopper hops, saying 'Join in the fun!'
While the branches all twist, shy from the sun.
They laugh in the breeze as they sway to the sound,
In a world full of laughter, it's joy that they found.

Crispy Retreats

In the crunch of autumn's breath,
I find a cozy place,
Where branches wave their greeting,
And nature sets the pace.

Oh, the squirrels play their games,
Chasing shadows with delight,
While I sip my cider dreams,
And think of what feels right.

A gust of wind, a rustle loud,
As if they scheme and plot,
To toss me into their fun,
But I'm the calmer spot.

So here I sit, content to stay,
With laughter in my heart,
Let all those branches dance away,
I've got my crunch to start.

Colors of Quiet Rebellion

Beneath the boughs where whispers live,
A riot of shades unfolds,
Crimson, amber, gold, and green,
Nature's tale retold.

The leaves are flipping up their skirts,
Twirling with a grin,
One says, 'Join our merry dance,'
But I'm no fool to spin.

Chasing dreams in swirl and spin,
While others join the fun,
I'll stay put, my drink in hand,
Let them dance and run.

For every twirl and sneaky jump,
In silence, I will reign,
Cheers to colors wild and bright,
Oh, freedom without pain!

The Silence Beneath the Canopy

The trees are quiet, shushing loud,
With secrets intertwined,
I peek beneath the leafy crown,
To what's in store to find.

A squirrel sweeps his nutty stash,
While robins sing their tune,
But I'm wrapped in peace and shade,
Underneath the afternoon.

In this tranquil wooden space,
I don't need any chat,
While others laugh and chatter on,
I simply tip my hat.

So let the woodland loudly play,
My heart's a gentle beat,
Let them jump and sway about,
I'm here, and I'm discreet.

Glimmers of Separation

The sun ignites the world with gold,
As branches wave goodbye,
I watch them scatter 'round and round,
And let out a soft sigh.

Flamboyant colors drift away,
Like confetti in the breeze,
But here beneath this cozy arc,
I enjoy my own tease.

My friends can play their little games,
I'll nibble on my snack,
With every flutter, sway, and twirl,
I'm glad I stayed intact.

So let them flutter far and wide,
I'll keep my laughter near,
With every glow of separation,
I'm mastering good cheer.

Unspoken Prayers of the Forest Floor

In whispers low, the leaves they sigh,
Beneath my feet, they wave goodbye.
Joking softly, they start to tease,
"Would you like a salad with that breeze?"

Dancing shadows, they shimmy and sway,
"Not today, I've got plans to play!"
The forest floor chuckles with cheer,
"Take a hike, we're staying right here!"

Pine cones laugh as they tumble down,
While acorns giggle without a frown.
"You can't catch us, we're not your snack!"
On woodland paths, they plan their attack.

So join the fun, don't take it slow,
The ground is alive with nature's show.
Laughter echoes through trees so tall,
In the chatty woods, it's a ball after all!

Touching the Silence of Decay

In the quiet shade where fungi bloom,
A mushroom jokes, "I'm here for the gloom!"
With each slow fade, the laughter grows,
"It's not just dirt, it's comedy shows!"

Twisted branches fight for the light,
"Why so serious? Let's take flight!"
When autumn calls with colors bold,
The trees spin tales that never get old.

Beneath the crunch of the fallen kind,
The snickering snails leave jokes behind.
"Has anyone seen my silent retreat?"
Through decay's humor, life is sweet!

So while we roam on this aging ground,
Let's tap our toes to the rustling sound.
In whispers of change, let laughter spark,
For even in silence, there's joy in the dark!

Echoes in the Canopy

In the woods, a bird does squawk,
"Please don't make the branches rock!"
Squirrels chatter, oh what a tease,
"Back off, buddy, I need some cheese!"

The sun peeks through, a sunlit grin,
Trees giggle, they revel in sin.
"Can't you see, we need some space?"
"Buzz off, bug! You're in the wrong place!"

Tired of Treetops

The branches sway, tired to their core,
"Must you stomp? We can't take much more."
A raccoon naps in a leafy retreat,
"Do you mind? I'm trying to sleep!"

Birds play tag with the breeze outside,
"Hey, watch it! We're here for the ride."
They tussle and tumble, stick to their game,
"Keep it down! We're all feeling the same."

Embrace the Rustle

Leaves giggle in the brisk cold air,
"Not us again! We've got roots to share."
A woeful branch whispers with sass,
"Please shoo away that pesky grass!"

Wind whispers secrets, both cheeky and sly,
"Why so serious? Just let it fly!"
Nature's punchline, a comedic twist,
"Leaf us be, we're hard to resist!"

Moments of Verdant Solace

In the shade, we're making a pact,
"No more noise, that's a fact!"
Dancing shadows on a sunny day,
"Join in fun or be on your way!"

Breezes carry laughter up high,
As fluttering petals begin to sigh.
"Just chill, friend, let's take a break,
Turn up the mirth, for goodness' sake!"

Where the Green Turns Grassy

In the garden, I once sat,
With a squirrel, wearing a hat.
He stole my sandwich, such a brat,
Now he's chubby, just like that.

The flowers whisper tales so grand,
While the weeds, they take a stand.
Dancing to a tune unplanned,
They're the rebels of this land.

A butterfly flits by my cheek,
Its wings are bold, but what a sneak.
It lands right on my sandwich peak,
I chase it off with a loud squeak.

Amidst the grass, I find my peace,
In chaos, nature finds its tease.
With giggles, my worries cease,
In the green, there's such release.

Prayers of a Withering Oak

Oh mighty oak, so wise and grand,
You've watched my folly, my clumsy hand.
With leaves that drift like grains of sand,
Your branches dance, a tired band.

I pray for strength to hold on tight,
But squirrels mock me, what a sight!
They jest and leap, so full of might,
While I just sway, a sorry plight.

Under your shade, I often nap,
While birds above conspire, perhaps.
Would trade my roots for a cookie flap,
As laughter fills the leafy gap.

Oh oak, your charm I can't resist,
With every branch, a twist of bliss.
But if you act like this persists,
You'll find my lunch is on your list!

A Lament for Lost Greenery

Once a garden, now a mess,
Where thorny weeds began to press.
My flowers wilted, I must confess,
As grass grows wild in its excess.

The daisies roll their eyes in vain,
While dandelions sing in rain.
Oh what a silly plant campaign,
They giggle, causing me such pain.

A lost race, I shout in jest,
Against the chaos, I must protest.
Yet every bloom, I still invest,
In garden battles, I'm the guest.

So here I stand, a hero brave,
Among the green, no time to cave.
Embracing chaos, that's the rave,
What once was neat, now wild and grave!

Serenity Found in Detached Shades

Chillin' beneath a shady tree,
A leaf falls down and scolds me, see?
It's lost its grip, it's feeling free,
While I just wish for harmony.

The branches stretch, they sway and bend,
As shadows play, they're quite the trend.
In this retreat, I find a friend,
The grass below, it has no end.

A cricket chirps a silly beat,
As ants march by, with little feet.
In nature's joke, I take my seat,
Life's comedy is ever sweet.

So let them flutter, fall, and float,
In every breeze, a funny note.
For in this bliss where all can gloat,
Detached from stress, I breathe, I quote!

Fragments of Color in a Hectic World

In the park, a squirrel prances,
Chasing shadows, taking chances.
A vibrant leaf slips from a tree,
"Catch me!" it seems to plea.

Bouncing around like it's alive,
Dancing as if on a hive.
The world spins fast, yet here it glows,
While busy folks just rush and go.

Children giggle, dogs do bark,
Amidst the chaos, life's a lark.
Yet autumn says, "Hey, take a seat!"
As colors fall, a wild retreat.

So grab a brew, and settle down,
Watch the leaves, a playful crown.
In this frantic, swirling race,
Each leaf a joke, a warm embrace.

Seeds of Solitude

In the garden, a lone seed sighs,
Dreaming big, under blue skies.
It giggles at the bustling throng,
"Why in a hurry? Come sing my song!"

A raindrop teases with a tickle,
As bees buzz by, oh what a fickle!
"I'm just a seed, don't drag me out!"
It murmurs soft, without a doubt.

The world's a circus, wild and loud,
But this little seed is oh so proud.
Content to burrow in the ground,
Where silence reigns, and peace is found.

Whispers of roots, a quiet hymn,
A solitary dance, on a whim.
In every crack and crevice deep,
The seed finds joy, the world can sleep.

Beneath the Boughs of Farewell

Under branches, shadows play,
A gentle breeze, it steals away.
Leaves drop down, a cheeky jest,
"It's time for naps, you need some rest!"

As folks walk by with hurried frowns,
I laugh aloud, while leafing towns.
"Why rush your steps, when I can float?"
Each leaf takes flight, a funny quote.

Beneath the boughs, I sit and grin,
Nature's comedy, let's begin!
A tumble here, a pirouette there,
I'm the king of this leafy fare.

So take a break from daily grind,
Underneath, a treasure find!
With twirls and swirls, we bid adieu,
Join the fun, it's all for you!

Frayed Edges of Time

Time frays at corners, soft and sweet,
Like an old leaf caught under feet.
"Hey, watch it!" it whispers low,
As memories dance and ebb and flow.

Tick-tock goes the sneaky clock,
As laughter echoes, a playful shock!
With every rustle, time takes its flight,
Fleeting moments, oh what a sight!

A bird swoops down, a hat to steal,
While rustling leaves begin to squeal.
"Chase me now, or just unwind!"
As days run by, the joy we find.

So gather 'round, let stories bloom,
In frayed edges, there's always room.
For laughter lives beyond the bend,
Just grab a leaf, and call it friend!

Memories Beneath the Canopy

Under the branches, I took my stand,
Tickling leaves that danced hand in hand.
Whispers of stories from bark to root,
Yet all I can grasp is a floating seed's loot.

Dancing in circles, they fall with a swirl,
Each little twirl makes my head want to whirl.
"Catch me!" they giggle, as I try to engage,
Yet I'm just a guest in their leafy stage.

Fingers are slippery, I slip on a twig,
Wobbling around like a poorly tied jig.
Giggles erupt from the rustling leaves,
As I lose my balance, forget my reprieves.

A crown of green chips, now stuck in my hair,
Nature's confetti, with sass in the air.
With every misstep, they laugh in delight,
Beneath this tall canopy, life feels just right.

Tranquil Circles in the Gritty Tangle

In the chaos of underbrush, I search for a path,
Tangled and twisted – nature's math.
Each step is a dance with roots and weeds,
Tripping on laughter, forgetting my needs.

Squirrels are giggling, chubby-cheeked jesters,
Chasing their tails like clumsy investors.
I try to keep up, but they sprout wings,
While I'm stuck in boots with antiquated strings.

Joy of discovery: a rock shaped like cheese,
I grin at the thought, then I'm down on my knees.
Puddles reflecting the sky's silly grin,
Every leap closer brings me back to the spin.

Wandering gnomes wear hats made of grass,
I join their parade, feeling quite the ass.
Beneath every shadow, each quirky bend,
I'm at home in the chaos; let the fun never end!

The Secret Life of Severed Stems

In a jar on my desk, they sway and they wave,
Telling their tales of how they were brave.
Chopped from their homes, they now sit in style,
With roots that are feelers, making me smile.

As petals gossip with each daring twist,
I worry they're plotting to make me desist.
"Just give us water!" they chant with a cheer,
But who're they to judge my sip of cold beer?

Sunshine a treat, they lean in so bold,
Yet wilt with the hint of neglect, I'm told.
But tut-tut to dullness, let's dance on the rim,
I'm joining their waltz till the twilight grows dim.

Night falls with laughter, my plants start to sway,
With whispers of summers not scattered away.
We'll dream of green gardens while blooming in dreams,
What secret life thrives beneath playful beams?

Glistening Embers of Autumn's End

The breeze gives a chuckle, a zesty farewell,
To colorful crunches that soon will repel.
Dancing in spirals, those crisp little rascals,
Brittle but witty – their laughter unmasked souls.

Pumpkin parade makes a grand little scene,
Each patch full of mirth and hues of bright sheen.
Squash on the sidelines, they nod with delight,
As I prance through the foliage, feeling quite spright.

Squirrels in costume, adorned with acorns,
Pretending they're kings of this woodland norm.
I join in their jest, tippy-toeing near,
To snag a few chuckles from autumns so clear.

We gather our treasures, nature's last cheer,
As the moon crowns the night, casting laughter and fear.
With embers still glowing, we bid our adieu,
To a season of fun, I'll return to renew.

Retreating Under Branches

In the shade where critters play,
I dodge the sun all day.
Whispers of the breeze so cool,
I'm just a leaf, avoiding school.

The squirrels laugh as I stay low,
Hiding from bright rays aglow.
A game of peek-a-boo I thrive,
It's my mission to survive.

Whispers of the Unseen

Amongst the twigs, I overhear,
All the gossip, quite the cheer!
A flutter here, a rustle there,
Nature's secrets fill the air.

Funny how they think I'm shy,
Just trying not to say goodbye.
Chirps and chuckles, quite the scene,
I'm the quiet one, unseen!

An Orchard of Isolation

In a world of fruits so bright,
I blend in, a leafy sight.
All around, they're in their zone,
I've made the branches my throne.

The apples chat, the berries tease,
While I sway in my own breeze.
"Come play!" they call with sunny smiles,
But I'm too busy with my styles.

The Flurry of a Farewell

Wind picks up, oh what a race,
With swirling leaves, I lose my place.
Twisting, turning in the air,
Adieu to all, with flair and care.

So here I go, a whirlwind show,
Off I drift, as breezes blow.
Laughter follows as I twirl,
An exit leaf that makes the world swirl!

A Symphony of Surrendered Green

The branches wave, a playful tease,
As I dodge the rain of leafy sneeze.
Oh, why do you flutter, O vibrant hue,
I promise, I'm not playing peek-a-boo!

The garden's a stage, the trees take flight,
While I stand here, a hapless sight.
You dance around, just let me be,
I'm trying to sip my herbal tea!

They giggle and whisper with every gust,
Each rustle a joke; they're full of trust.
With every flutter, my patience wears thin,
I ask for peace, but it's an endless din!

So here I sit, in leafy ballet,
With roots of laughter, they're not far away.
Oh nature, I'm begging, can't we atone?
For just one moment, let me alone!

Twilight Beneath the Dominant Oak

Oh mighty oak, in sunset's glow,
You shake your branches, putting on a show.
With every breath, your leaves do glee,
But they forget, I need to pee!

The squirrels are chattering, such a racket,
Dancing like they're in a wild bracket.
I just want silence, a moment to relax,
Instead I'm treated to acorn attacks!

Twilight's here, the shadows wane,
Your leafy laughter drives me insane.
With every creak, you play your tune,
I think I need a nice afternoon!

Oh twilight's creeping, will it ever cease?
Beneath your branches, I seek sweet peace.
A symphony of rustles, too loud to ignore,
Let me find calm on this forest floor!

The Last Dance of Whirling Colors

Oh, autumn's fringe, you're quite a sight,
But your swirling leaves cause quite a fright.
With every gust, they twirl and twist,
And I wish they'd simply be missed!

They spin like dancers, so full of flair,
My hat is gone! Should I really care?
The colors whirl, a circus act,
Each plummeting leaf is an ambush tactic!

I duck and weave in this vibrant storm,
While nature's set turns rather warm.
A final dance before they fall,
Why must your colors have a brawl?

The ground's now a patchwork, soft and loud,
I question my sanity, feeling quite bowed.
Oh, these whimsical pranks that the trees have thrust,
I just want to sit, without the fuss!

Untamed Silence Beneath the Elms

Under elms that sway and sway,
I seek some peace, but they just play.
Their branches wave in a raucous jest,
For silence, I seem to be a pest!

I rest my head, but here comes a breeze,
And all those leaves, they wail with ease.
I laugh along, though it starts to grind,
Oh, how I wish for a tranquil mind!

With acorns raining like someone's prank,
My nap is interrupted, my patience sank.
They rustle, they tussle, what's your plea?
I'm only trying to sip my iced tea!

Gentle elms, must you be so spry?
I'm just a poet, too weary to lie.
In this untamed theater, I plead my case,
For just a moment of gentle grace!

Stillness in the Afterglow

Sunset whispers through the trees,
Pushing shadows with a tease.
Branches sway as if to jest,
"Hey you! Just let me rest!"

Crickets joke in fading light,
Their chirps a comical plight.
Leaves giggle at the soft breeze,
"Can't you see? We need to sneeze!"

Squirrels chuckle, nuts in tow,
Hiding treasures in the glow.
Nature's laughter fills the air,
"Can you find me? Good luck there!"

Moonlight spills like shiny sparks,
As if it's tossing playful marks.
In this silence, hear the glee,
Nature's humor, wild and free!

Hymns of the Sheltering Boughs

Underneath the leafy shade,
Frogs croak tunes that never fade.
Their ribbits rise in merry chorus,
"Join us now, come sing before us!"

Fluttering wings and chirps collide,
Birds are laughing, full of pride.
"Guess who's got the bigger nest?
Spoiler—it's me, I'm the best!"

A bear wanders, feeling bold,
Tries to dance but plays too old.
Trees are swaying, giggling low,
"Look at him! What a show!"

As twilight wraps the world in gray,
The boughs hum tales from day to day.
In this forest, fun's never done,
With every stitch, we've just begun!

The Unraveled Threads of Chlorophyll

In the garden, green threads swap,
Colors dance and flowers hop.
A spider weaves a web with flair,
"I'm the artist, beware, beware!"

Roots entangle, plotting schemes,
Buried secrets, childish dreams.
"Catch me if you think you're quick,
But I'm hiding with a trick!"

Worms converse in silly tones,
Making jokes about their bones.
"I've got the best soil recipe,
Want to share? Come play with me!"

Amidst the blooms and buzzing bees,
Nature's laughter floats like breeze.
With every giggle, every sound,
Magic in the muck is found!

Whispered Thoughts in the Gnarled Roots

Twisted roots whisper secrets tight,
"Did you hear what the owl said last night?"
Branches lean in, eager to know,
"Spill the tea, put on a show!"

Chirpy beetles join the fun,
Rolling around, oh, what a run!
"Catch me, catch me," they taunt and tease,
"Try and find us—it's a breeze!"

The old oak chuckles, wise and stout,
"Life's a game, go on, shout!"
Leaves ruffle in agreement true,
"Guess who's winning? Well, it's you!"

As twilight drapes the cozy grove,
Friends gather 'round, feeling the love.
In the roots that twist and turn,
Laughter's lessons we all learn!

Conversations with the Wind

Oh Wind, you tickle my nose,
With whispers of nonsense, I suppose.
You tease the trees that sway and dance,
Making each branch seem like it has a chance.

You carry my thoughts, up high they soar,
Then drop them like crumbs, right by my door.
A gusty giggle, a playful nudge,
We trade our secrets, won't you budge?

Your breath is a prank, a cheeky bluff,
You ruffle my hair, oh that's quite enough!
But in your presence, I can't help but smile,
Even as you whisk my papers a mile.

So talk to me, Wind, let's share some fun,
We'll dance in circles till the day is done.
I won't be bothered, just stay awhile,
For every breeze carries a hint of guile.

In the Thicket of Thoughts

In tangled thoughts, I'm lost, you see,
Like vines entwined, they won't set me free.
I ponder and sigh, with a whimsical frown,
As bushes giggle at my mental breakdown.

Each twig a notion, each leaf a scheme,
I chase them around like it's one big dream.
But they rustle away, those pesky ideas,
Like squirrels with acorns, all full of sneers!

I shout at the branches, 'Can't you be clear?'
But they just chuckle, 'We don't shed a tear!'
I'm stuck here, dancing in my fantasy realm,
While shadows play keepers at their leafy helm.

So here I will sit, in this leafy maze,
With thoughts swirling 'round in a dizzying daze.
A giggle escapes, as I tip my hat,
To the thicket of thoughts, imagine that!

A Solitary Journey Through the Grove

In the grove I wander, all alone,
With trees as my companions, made of stone.
They stand so tall, with roots dug deep,
Whispering tales in a hushed, slow creep.

I wave to a trunk, but it just stays still,
'No fun in chatting, just a wooden thrill.'
A hollow log laughs, its sound rings true,
Echoing my jokes, as if it knew!

I stumble on branches, tripping with glee,
The ground laughs too, with a ticklish spree.
Each pebble is chuckling, every leaf has a grin,
As I strut through the grove, delighted within.

So here I will roam among my stoic friends,
Sharing my giggles as this journey bends.
A merry old trek, just me and the trees,
Creating my laughter, carried on the breeze.

Gently Unraveled by the Breeze

A gentle breeze whips through the park,
It curls around me, playful and stark.
It gives my hat a little spin,
And tickles my cheeks, a cheeky win!

It sweeps my worries right off the path,
With every gust, it ignites a laugh.
The flowers sway with a teasing nod,
As I dance along, quite unflawed!

I shout, 'Oh breeze, can you stay a bit?'
But it swirls away, not a moment to sit.
Like a silly friend, it bounces and plays,
Inviting me to join in its maze.

So I twirl and giggle, letting go of the day,
As the breeze whisks my troubles away,
With each little dance, my heart starts to rise,
Unraveled, I'm free, beneath open skies.

The Space Between Green

In the garden, a whispering breeze,
Dares to tease amongst the trees.
A succulent leaf hides with glee,
Yelling, "Don't bother! Let me be!"

Sunlight giggles, casting shadows,
Tickling trunks with playful throes.
But that cheeky vine doesn't retreat,
Swaying to rhythms that can't be beat.

Sassy petals sway with flair,
Announcing loudly, "Please, just beware!"
Gossip gathers on a high branch,
As lone leaves plot their grand expanse.

Frogs croak loudly with a jest,
"We're roommates now, this is a fest!"
Every rustle tells a tall tale,
In this leafy dance, we'll never fail.

Shades of Discontent

In a tangled mess of colors bright,
A stubborn leaf puts up a fight.
Tired of swaying, it claims it's king,
While the breeze just laughs, "What a thing!"

Barking at worms with a sassy flair,
"It's my turf, so how do you dare?"
Playing hide and seek among the blooms,
Whispering secrets and nursery tunes.

The daisies chuckle, the roses roll eyes,
As the leaf grumbles, stuck in disguise.
"Oh to be free," it pines with a grin,
As if standing still is a fun little win.

While clouds drift by, all fluff and winks,
That leaf sighs deeply and often thinks,
Maybe the grass should have a turn,
In this silly game, when will it learn?

Detachment in Decay

Once vibrant hues now fragile and frail,
An old leaf dances, a tired tale.
Hanging on tight, it gives a tease,
"Catch me if you can, oh gentle breeze!"

"Lloyd, let's go!" a nearby twig chimes,
But the leaf just mumbles, "Not now, good times."
Fading and flipping with theatrical flair,
Declaring, "I'm the star of this air!"

An acorn snickers, "You're just a husk!
Why hold on tight when you're full of dust?"
The leaf responds with sarcasm so dry,
"Every girl has her turn to fly!"

So they giggle silently, nature's own jest,
In the throes of decay, they feel truly blessed.
Sitting in stillness, a reluctant parade,
"Here's to the end, let's all be remade!"

The Echoing Rustle

A sound of mischief, a playful rustle,
Leaves declare war in a leafy tussle.
Whispers of laughter float on the air,
"Just trying to chill, if you care!"

Branches elope, they sway to the beat,
While squirrels debate who will take a seat.
One leaf boasts, "You can count on me,
To make rustling sounds, oh so free!"

Who knew that foliage had so much fun?
Each snap and crackle like a pun.
The repetition in the whispering shades,
Echoes in laughter, as friendship invades.

So let's gather round, in this leafy affair,
With tickling breezes that tousle our hair.
In the forest's embrace, we find our song,
In this rustling world, we're never wrong!

Whispering Canopies

Up in the branches, squirrels play,
Chasing their tails in a leafy ballet.
They giggle and squeak, such raucous cheer,
While I sip my tea, wishing they'd disappear.

Fluttering leaves drop, making a show,
Like nature's confetti, a vibrant throw.
But when they cling, oh, what a surprise!
It's a foliage party right on my thighs!

The wind starts to swirl, leaves twist in a jest,
Hiding my snacks like a leafy protest.
I turn with a laugh, brush them away,
Those mischievous greens in their grand display.

So here I sit, in my leafy retreat,
Laughing aloud at the furry elite.
In this wild woodland, let giggles ensue,
As the trees roll their eyes, "What more can we do?"

Solitude Among the Foliage

In my quiet spot, the trees stand tall,
Branches waving gently, answering my call.
A rustle above makes me laugh in surprise,
"Oh, it's just a bird - but isn't it wise?"

Beneath the green quilt, I rest with a grin,
Nature's chorus around me, teasing within.
A worm wriggles past, with an air of great flair,
"Go on, buddy, just tread with some care!"

The shadows dance playfully, casting their tricks,
While I munch on acorns, enjoying my mix.
Autumn's chill whispers, with jokes of its own,
But I giggle back, for I'm never alone.

So here's to the greens, both the silly and sweet,
Who flutter and frolic at my grassy seat.
I'll enjoy this hush, with a wink and a cheer,
In this leafy solitude, there's nothing to fear.

Shadows of Autumn's Embrace

Dancing in shadows, the leaves spin around,
Flashing gold, red, and love without sound.
They tickle my shoulders, a whimsical game,
In this autumn ballet, I join in the fame.

"Hey, stop it!" I chuckle, swatting them away,
But they flutter and giggle, "Come join, it's okay!"
This playful parade takes me all by surprise,
As shadows become friends, in the dimming skies.

A gust of wind swoops, what capsizing fun!
I'm buried in colors, a vibrant rerun.
But I pop out with laughter, a clown in disguise,
With nature's parade sprinkling joy in my eyes.

So here in this ruckus, I'll dance and I'll play,
With shadows of autumn, come what may.
They whisper their secrets on breezy delight,
And I'll twirl with the trees, til the fall turns to night.

Rustling Silence

In the silent woods, I search for some peace,
But those rustling leaves never seem to cease.
They chatter and gossip with each little breeze,
While I'm trying to think, "Oh, can't you freeze?"

Sitting on soil, the laughter is loud,
A chorus of crickets, a leafy crowd.
"Excuse me," I shout, "could I get a break?"
But they giggle and squeal, for they're wide awake.

Flutter, whisper, ballet in the trees,
I grin at their antics, despite my unease.
In this quiet retreat, they're quite the jokers,
Nature's own comedians, flapping like brokers.

So I'll grab my snacks and join in the fun,
Rustling with laughter beneath the sun.
Surrounded by folly, I embrace every sound,
In the rustling silence, joyfully found.

Shadows Among the Shimmering Green

In a forest filled with chatter,
The branches dance and sway.
I wave to the busy critters,
Then hide and hope they stay!

The sunlight laughs with dainty rays,
Daring my shadow to play.
But I just want to lounge around,
And nap the afternoon away!

The rustling leaves are gossiping,
About my lazy spree.
Yet here I am, just chilling out,
Drinking snacks, fancy-free.

So if you seek me in the woods,
I'm not behind the trees.
I'm somewhere making memories,
With squirrels and honeybees!

Quest for Quiet in a World of Color

Oh, the hues are loud and bright,
Like a kid with too much cake.
I seek a soft and gentle spot,
    For a cozy little break.

The flowers flaunt their vivid dresses,
    Parading in the sun.
While I just want to curl up tight,
And not join their colorful fun!

The birds sing opera in the trees,
    It's a cacophony, I say!
While I'm here in my little nook,
    Dreaming the day away.

So hush, you shades of bold and brash,
    Let me catch some peace!
I just need a minute, please,
For this vibrant chaos to cease!

The Art of Letting Go

I drop my worries with the leaves,
A gentle autumn breeze.
They twirl and swirl to ground below,
Just like my restless knees.

The branches stretch to bid goodbye,
To all their twinkling gems.
I giggle as I toss away,
My burdens like old pens.

The squirrels watch with beady eyes,
As I let out a cheer.
Who knew letting go could be,
A party of the year?

So come and join my merry dance,
Where worries hit the floor,
For in this art of letting go,
We'll laugh forevermore!

Solitary Sighs Under the Maple

With branches wide, the maple sighs,
   A whisper soft and sweet.
I take a seat, my favorite nook,
   Where calm and giggles meet.

The wind drags secrets from the sky,
   And tickles leafless ghosts.
They swirl around like playful sprites,
   Good company, at most!

I ponder life, or maybe snack,
   With laughter as my muse.
For lonely moments under trees,
   Are blissfully my chosen views!

So here I sit, just me and dreams,
   The world can buzz with glee.
I'll dwell in solace with my thoughts,
   While sipping nature's tea!

Treading Quietly on the Golden Path

I tiptoe lightly on my way,
Hoping no one sees me stray.
The crunch beneath my careful feet,
Oh, what a funny little treat!

A squirrel stares with knowing eyes,
As if to shout, "Surprise, surprise!"
I jump and giggle, dart away,
And leave my worries where they lay.

The sunbeams dance through branches high,
While autumn whispers, "Do not try!"
I dance and twirl, quite unaware,
Of golden treasures everywhere.

But lo and behold, with each new step,
I find a treasure that I kept.
A snap, a crack, it's clear to see,
Nature's gift is fun for me!

A Journey Through Verdant Repose

In fields of green I roam and prance,
With every shiver, a silly dance.
Leaves tickle toes, it's all in fun,
As bugs applaud my little run.

I stumble upon a playful breeze,
It swirls around, oh, how it teases!
A grassy tickle, I laugh out loud,
Turning me into a giggling crowd.

I take a moment just to sigh,
A cloud drifts past, it looks so shy.
I wave hello, it puffs and flows,
Chasing shadows where no one goes.

But nature's jest has one more play,
A hidden puddle sets the day.
Splash and giggle, I'm soaked anew,
In verdant glee, oh what a view!

In the Echo of Crumbling Petals

As petals fall with gentle grace,
I pretend it's a flower race.
Each color spins in dizzy delight,
Turning the mundane day to night.

I take a bow and spin around,
The petals swirl in merry sound.
Who knew a garden could be so fun?
Like a carnival under the sun!

A bee buzzes near, it seems to cheer,
As I twirl about without a fear.
"Join the dance!" I say to the bug,
While it fumbles, my heart gives a shrug.

With laughter loud, I greet the breeze,
It turns my giggle into a tease.
Petals rain down, a floral rain,
In this lively jest, I'm never plain!

Shadows of the Sun-Kissed Wood

In the shadows of a leafy dome,
I feel a giggle start to roam.
Squirrels scamper, branches sway,
What a joyous, frolicsome display!

The dappled light plays peek-a-boo,
With every step, it laughs anew.
Each twist and turn, a chuckle near,
The whispers fill the air with cheer.

But look out, here comes a sneaky breeze,
It raises leaves like it's a tease.
I jump back quick, almost in flight,
And land in shadows, what a sight!

In the sun-kissed wood where laughter lies,
Where every stumble leads to surprise,
I dance among the leafy friends,
In this silly world, the fun never ends!

A Fall from Grace

In the park, I tripped on a twirl,
A tumble that made my heart whirl.
Leaves chuckled, as they danced by,
I swear they winked, oh me, oh my!

With every flop, a new leaf jests,
They gather round for a giggle fest.
I try to rise with humorous flair,
But alas, I'm flat—stuck in mid-air!

Gusty breezes tease and they poke,
As they rustle, they whisper—a joke!
Every tumble, a new punchline found,
In the world of leaves, I'm the clown unbound!

I waddle away, much to their glee,
Next time, I swear, just let me be!
With every step, I sketch a new jest,
In this leafy dance, I surely am blessed!

Quietude in the Grove

In the grove, there's silence so neat,
But the leaves conspire, oh, what a feat!
Whispers float like a soft, gentle tease,
They giggle away on a playful breeze.

I'd seek a refuge, just me and my space,
Yet these pranks feel like a sweet embrace.
Squirrels plot, the leaves flick and spin,
Another day, let the antics begin!

Underfoot, a rustle, a sudden surprise,
Nature's joke lands right on my thighs.
A giggling chorus of rustling sighs,
"Leave it to us, to entertain skies!"

So I smile, I chuckle, amidst the game,
In the quietude, they're never the same.
With every rustling, I'm caught in the whim,
In this fun grove, I won't let it dim!

Nature's Plea for Distance

Nature beckons, her arms wide in cheer,
Yet closer I come—she lets out a sneer.
"Back off a tad!" the branches declare,
"Your presence, dear friend, is far too rare!"

Blades of grass giggle, a teasing brigade,
For the closer I stroll, the more they invade.
Each leaf whispers a soft, sly plea,
"Can we have a moment of nature's decree?"

I backpedal slowly, take heed of the call,
But nature's whispers, they echo and sprawl.
With every step, they fall and they sway,
"Your company's nice, but here's our ballet!"

The creatures giggle, they twist and they twine,
In nature's plea, I can't help but divine,
"Laugh with us now, take heed of the prance,
For distance is fun in this leafy romance!"

Barking Up the Wrong Tree

I ventured out, with grand plans in mind,
But trees and their leaves had trouble aligned.
I trekked on the path, feeling quite bold,
When I bumped one and later felt old.

"Hey buddy, who let you in our midst?"
They whispered and giggled with every twist.
I shrugged it off, was ready to flee,
But they tugged at my sleeve, saying, "Stay with me!"

Squirrels laughed loudly, they howled with delight,
As I stumbled 'round, oh what a sight!
Branches shook hands with leaves in a twist,
Whimsical wonders I couldn't resist!

So here I remain, amidst whimsy and cheer,
Barking up treetops, I've nothing to fear.
I enter the fray, with jokes all around,
In this frolicsome nature, joy's always found!

The Hidden Note Beneath the Boughs

In the shade where whispers play,
A note was hidden, come what may.
It asked me kindly, quite sincere,
To take a walk and shed my fear.

I grabbed my hat and danced around,
But leaves were laughing, what a sound!
They rustled jokes, my heart was light,
As I engaged in this leafly flight.

Chasing Shadows of Summer's End

The sun dips low, a golden thief,
I chase its rays, yet find mischief.
A shadow flirts, it slips away,
   Is it a leaf or just a play?

I run and tumble, twist and spin,
"What's the rush?" the leaves begin.
They chuckle softly, just let be,
As autumn yawns and smiles at me.

Surrendering to the Cycle

When colors clash in wild array,
I ponder life, then grand ballet.
The leaves take flight, a dance divine,
While squirrels prance, they sip their wine.

I yield to whims, like twirling leaf,
Embracing joy, rejecting grief.
In nature's grip, I laugh and spin,
For every loss, there's room to win.

The Art of Disappearing Foliage

With every breeze, a game of hide,
The leaves perform, they've got great pride.
Below my feet, a crunchy sound,
As if the earth is joyously bound.

They comb the ground, a painted maze,
Turning heads in so many ways.
I giggle at this leafy jest,
Who needs green? This hues the best!

Moments of Breath Among the Splintered Stems

In the garden of shadows, I tread with glee,
Dodging the prickle of branches set free.
A dance with the weeds, a jig up the trail,
Laughter erupts like a soft morning gale.

Petals go flying, a wild, sunny crowd,
Nature's confetti, my heart feeling proud.
The sun's rays are tickling, I've lost all my cares,
Perhaps I'll just stay, whisper secrets to flares.

Enjoying this riot of green and of brown,
Why leave the frolic when I'm wearing a crown?
A butterfly winks; we're both on a spree,
Shhh! Don't tell the flowers, they're minding their tea.

So dance with me here, we'll waltz through the blades,
Until afternoon stirs, and the sun slowly fades.
I'll catch all the breezes, befriend all the flies,
Together as fools 'neath the vast open skies.

Surrender of the Splendid Shades

In a vibrant patchwork of petals and leaf,
I hide from my worries, oh sweet, sweet relief.
The squirrels are plotting, their antics absurd,
Chasing their tails, not a space left unstirred.

Under the arches where sunlight does pour,
I ponder my choices among limbs I adore.
With each little rustle, the forest will beckon,
A giggle escapes, wait—did that branch just reckon?

The ferns start to whisper their secrets to me,
"Join us in joy, let imagination run free!"
I'll flop like a fish or bounce like a bee,
In surrender of shades, you've got to agree!

So come take a moment, find laughter in gloom,
Among splashes of green, watch the smiles bloom.
Life's a silly dance, just embrace all its charms,
As nature spreads joy in her warm, leafy arms.

Exhaling Quietude from the Upper Boughs

Up high in the branches, I breathe in with cheer,
The sound of their rustling, so musical, dear.
A robin is crooning a tune full of zest,
I might stay forever, this cocoon feels the best.

Clouds drift like dreamers, so carefree and light,
They giggle at me as they float out of sight.
In moment's embrace, I lean back and grin,
What mischief arise when the winds begin!

From the tops of this haven, I gaze at the ground,
A kingdom of creatures, let's hear their sweet sound!
The ants hold a meeting; the grasshoppers play,
Join me in laughter—come, let's seize the day!

With echoes of quietude, magic does weave,
There's much to discover if only we leave!
So here in these branches, let joy be the thought,
In the rustle of leaves, laughter is sought.

Hiding in Dappled Shadows

In the twist of the tree limbs, I've found a sly spot,
Where sunlight and laughter dance bright on the dot.
The playful of shadows, they whisper and tease,
"Lounge with us now, put your mind at ease!"

Through the dappled green light, I peek with delight,
A jester of nature, I chuckle in bright.
With foxes and rabbits conspiring with me,
To craft silly schemes over cups of mint tea.

While daydreams dash by like butterflies' flight,
I banter with blooms until falls into night.
Their petals, they giggle, they flop and they sway,
"Don't rush to escape, stay and laugh through the day!"

"So hide in our shadows, we'll sound the loud cheer,
For moments of stillness bring joy that is clear.
In dappled embrace, where the laughter will call,
We'll dance in these rays, let the shadows enthrall!"

Wanderlust in the Dappled Light

Sunlight filters through the trees,
Casting shapes that dance with ease.
My shoes are tied, my heart's aglow,
For adventures where the wild winds blow.

A squirrel waves, I wave back slow,
Chasing dreams where zany breezes blow.
I trip on roots, but hey, that's fate,
Embrace the tumble; it's never too late.

The path is quirky, the shades are bright,
With nature's giggles, it feels just right.
A wanderer's heart, forever it roams,
In hues of green, I make my homes.

So let's frolic beneath this sky,
Among the branches, oh me, oh my!
Adventure's call is clear as day,
In dappled light, I'll dance and sway.

Only Silence Among the Twisted Branches

Under the boughs where critters peek,
Silence whispers, yet laughter's unique.
Talking trees share gossip's whim,
About the owl who lost a limb.

The breeze tickles, rustles the leaves,
Fallen branches playing tricks, oh please!
Squirrels plotting their next heist,
Watch your nuts, or they'll be diced.

Amongst the twisters, secrets hide,
But every murmur, I abide.
Nature's jokes, oh what a feast,
Bringing joy, to say the least.

So quiet here, but oh so fun,
Amidst the branches, under the sun.
In tangled tales of silly glee,
It's laughter, really, that says "be free."

A Soliloquy of Fallen Colors

Crimson and gold upon the ground,
Whispering stories without a sound.
Each leaf a giggle, each twirl a dance,
Nature's palette, a romping romance.

Blowing kisses in the autumn air,
Scattering colors without a care.
In the crunching symphony that plays,
I join the leaves in their merry ballet.

With a twist and twirl, I join the fun,
Catching colors like they were a gun.
Launching laughter through the brisk sky,
As tumbleweeds tumble; oh, my oh my!

So here I stand, a confetti of hues,
Dancing with joy in this leafy muse.
A soliloquy, as bright as a star,
In the vibrant chaos, I'm never far.

The Unseen Path Beyond the Thorns

Overgrown trails hide behind the thicket,
Where the brave roam; they must be a bit wicked.
Thorns are the guards, keeping things sly,
Yet beyond their grasp, adventures lie.

I poke and prod, but with a grin,
As if these brambles were just a spin.
Dodging the prickles with wise old flair,
Every scratch reminds me I dare.

What's this? A glimpse of light peeking through?
A secret garden with skies so blue!
I leap and twirl, dance through the pain,
For glory awaits where the thorns wane.

So onward I march, past the scariest greens,
With brave little giggles and playful screams.
For in the unknown, laughter is found,
On unseen paths where joy is unbound.

Solace in the Falling Hues

A leaf has dropped and made a sound,
Someone's yelling from the ground.
"Don't you dare fall on my head!"
But it's just nature—go ahead!

The trees are laughing, what a sight!
As colors dance in pure delight.
They flutter down, they wiggle free,
It's just chaos—can't you see?

A gentle breeze gives a swift nudge,
"Come on, buddy, just hold a grudge!"
They twirl and spin in playful jest,
As if they're on a nature quest!

So grab your hat, take a stroll,
Let leaves go wild, that's the goal!
A comedy show of autumn's grace,
Where leaves take flight, it's a wild race!

Whispers from the Woodland Floor

A crunchy sound beneath my feet,
Nature's voice, a funny beat.
Look out, watch out, that leaf might bite!
Oh, what a ruckus, pure delight!

Among the trees, a giggle grows,
Why do they tease? Nobody knows!
Each leaf's a joker, full of fun,
Playing tricks until they're done!

Swirling in circles, round they sway,
In the wind, they laugh and play.
"Catch me if you can!" they yell,
Oh, woodland pranks, they cast a spell!

So wander on this forest floor,
Join the laughter, hear the roar!
Leaves with antics, wild and free,
This woodland dance, a jolly spree!

When Autumn Paints the Path

Autumn's here, what a grand show,
Paints the floor with hues that glow!
"Step right up, let's have some fun!"
Leaves leap around, a colorful run!

Walking past, I trip and slide,
Oh, what joy I cannot hide!
Each leaf's a smile; bright and bold,
Nature's laughter, never old!

A rustle here, a flutter there,
Leaves are plotting, do I dare?
To join their party, to spin and sway,
In this dance of the autumn day!

So grab a friend and come along,
Join the ruckus, join the song!
A parade of colors, vibrant and free,
When autumn walks, just follow me!

Hushed Wonders of the Wanderer

In my path, a leaf does prance,
"Watch your step, join the dance!"
A quiet giggle from behind—
Those leafy friends are quite unkind!

They rustle softly, plotting schemes,
"Just try to catch us!" in my dreams.
With every step, they twist and twirl,
Nature's clowns in a leafy whirl!

I scramble over, watch my shoe,
Each leaf a joker, that's my cue!
A tumble here, I start to laugh,
It's nature's way, no photograph!

So stroll along this forest lane,
With leaves that tease, no chance of pain!
In quiet woods, let laughter reign,
A whispered joke in autumn's lane!

The Quietude Beneath the Branches

In the shade, I find my peace,
Squirrels chatter, never cease.
A gentle breeze tickles the ground,
While I sip tea, all around.

Acorns drop with a tiny thud,
I'd rather stay than face the flood.
Conversations with bark seem wise,
Napping here is quite the prize!

Birds chirp gossip, sweet and clear,
I wave at clouds, they disappear.
Branches sway in a noble dance,
To join this fun, you need the chance!

A picnic blanket, snacks galore,
Nature's party, never a bore.
So join me here in this green retreat,
We'll giggle at life and share a treat!

When Green Turns to Gold

Autumn whispers in shades so bright,
Nature's jest in a colorful flight.
Yellow and orange, such a sight,
I chuckle at leaves taking their flight.

Falling softly like clumsy dancers,
Showing off their vibrant prancers.
While I sip my pumpkin brew,
Laughing at how they bid adieu.

Their crinkled forms tell tales of cheer,
As they float down without a fear.
I tip my hat to the sneaky breeze,
Who stirs this frolic with such ease.

Nature's jesters, take your bows,
You've stolen smiles and earned your wow.
In skirts of gold, they seem so bold,
As the winds gossip—stories retold!

Uninvited Musings Among the Roots

Beneath the soil, thoughts like tendrils creep,
While the sun above shines, and clouds peep.
Worms hold council, planning their schemes,
  Digging through dirt in ludicrous dreams.

Mossy carpets, oh so plush,
Tickle my knees, oh, what a rush!
I laugh at beetles, strutting their stuff,
In this underground club, it's never tough.

Rabbits gossip, furry and spry,
What's on the menu? A carrot pie!
I root for parties, deep in the dark,
Springtime whispers, it's time to spark!

So let them chatter in earthy delight,
As I chill here, with spirits so light.
With nature's jesters dancing around,
I enjoy the peace—no need to be found!

The Stillness of Decay

Crisp leaves crunch beneath my feet,
In this quiet dance, I take a seat.
Nature's snore is quite a sound,
As old tales of autumn swirl around.

With every crackle, laughter brews,
Old sounds of fall bring quirky hues.
Rustling whispers of history told,
While sipping cider, warmed from the cold.

Twigs poke fun at the fading bloom,
Wishing for spring in this cozy room.
Yet stillness here holds a charm,
With nature's humor, you can't do harm.

Now, I revel in this glorious decay,
Where jokes of seasons come out to play.
So let the world turn, as it may,
I'll sit here laughing, come what may!

www.ingramcontent.com/pod-product-compliance
Lightning Source LLC
Chambersburg PA
CBHW071834160426
43209CB00003B/290